Home Work

A Collection of Poems
Sparked by One White Woman's
Journey on the Matter of Race

Melissa Whiteford St. Clair

DEDICATION

Honoring the lives of five enslaved people.

Jane, Dina, Jess, Jean, and Jack.

ACKNOWLEDGEMENTS

In gratitude

To Kathy Goughenour, Business Coach and Trainer for Virtual Assistants who invited Lynne Hurdle Price, Conflict Resolution Strategist to speak to our Virtual Expert® Community about diversity, equity, and inclusion.

To Lynne Hurdle Price, Conflict Resolution Strategist for accepting me into her Level I group experience On The Matter Of Race: White People Committed to Beginning the Journey Together.

I took a journey I didn't have to think twice. I took a journey with my guide, Lynne Hurdle Price.

To my husband, Matt St. Clair, the first person to mention "doing something" with these words.

To my mentor, Patti Bozman for encouraging me to put together this book of work.

To my sounding board and my brother from another mother, Perry Jenkins.

To Pat Conroy and his beloved Beaufort, SC where I found inspiration as these words flowed into poetry.

Introduction

Home Work: A Collection of Poems Sparked by One White Woman's Journey on the Matter of Race was the product related to lessons and assignments while a participant in On The Matter of Race: White People Committed to Beginning the Journey Together, Level 1, September 2020 through February 2021.

Table of Contents

Unity Mural, Beaufort, SC

Harriet

State of Maryland, Dorchester County

On her head was a bounty

Be Free or Die

Across the miles, she did fly

Following the drinking gourd in the sky

11-6-2020

Beaufort, SC

Beaufort, SC the home
of Secession

Beaufort, SC the home
of Reconstruction - the
first chance for
change.

Living in this town of
juxtaposition, viewing
life through a broader
lens at close range.

10-3-2020

Awaken

Now is the time to awaken.

To equity forsaken.

The opportunity to right
wrongs.

Start a journey to sing a
freedom song.

Dismantle racism.

C'mon my friends let us
hack at the root.

Once you know, you know,
and I am resolute.

Our sisters and brothers
have been waiting too
long.

10-3-2020

To Harriet Tubman & Robert Smalls

You ran for your freedom with everything to
lose.

While I can't spend a day walking in your shoes

I hear your footfalls on the streets.

I follow your footsteps in unity and peace.

Racism to trample.

Thank you for your bravery and for leading by
example.

10-7-2020

Bust of Robert Smalls next to Tabernacle Baptist Church
and his burial place.

Appeal

2020 has made me ask

How long will social injustices continue to
last?

For you and your fellow wo/man you are
resistant to temporarily wear a mask

That could save your life, or the life of those
in your path.

You say, this pandemic, the squeeze, the
pressure, this precaution, is suffocating.

Think about George Floyd with a knee on his
neck, now that is suffocating.

White supremacy and white privilege are real.

Equality for all is an incredible ideal.

For everyone to be able to thrive, fully real.

I don't expect you to harken to my appeal.

But for just a few minutes stop and think how
it would feel

To free all people from this slithery eel.

Let's interrupt and stop the social injustice
reel!

It is truly America's Achilles heel

This is my humble appeal.

12-5-2020

Check Box

Check box for race

Check box for gender

People of Color were bought
and sold as legal tender.

A War between the States.

The systems have never
surrendered.

Institutions remain in place.

The guilty conscience of
white men to rid.

Let's work together to loosen
the lid,

No more to keep systemic
racism hid.

11-9-2020

White Fragility

Feeling my confusion and
oppression brought forth by a
pandemic

The suffocation of George
Floyd my eyes did see.

Not letting my White
Fragility

Which shows up in my
scripted, people-pleasing
personality

Keep me

From embarking on a journey

To learn more and advocate
for social justice and unity.

11-14-2020

Reconcile

I am white, the color
of oppression.

My face itself is a
microaggression.

Though I will never be
able to walk a mile

And conflict leaders
inform me to do more
than smile.

I am on a journey to
reconcile.

11-15-2020

What Being White Means to Me

Being white means to me

Bearing a color, I did not see.

Living a life of white privilege

My school years were spent deciding whether
to go or not to go to college.

As a young adult, I hung out with a group
of mixed races

I did not realize as we grew up our lives
were influenced by systems of varying
paces.

As a military family, we mingled with a
mixing bowl

Little did I know the continued damage of
years of injustice was taking a toll.

Witnessing a video of the murder by an
officer in blue of George Floyd.

Once I was awakened, I could no longer
avoid.

Ignorance is bliss.

I am leaning in, learning all I can about
systemic racism and how I can impact social
justice.

11-15-2020

Maryland, my Maryland

O say can you see.

Your anti-miscegenation law of 1681
established race categories.

Your efforts to "divide and conquer" –
lawmakers invented labels

To separate all working-class people who
could barely put food on their table.

By creating boxes based on color, white
supremacy did you enable.

The Founding Fathers took the next step in
1790 with the Naturalization Act to keep
white privilege intact.

The only persons who could apply for
citizenship were white, in fact.

Maryland, my Maryland

The Old Line State

Maryland, my Maryland

On 1 November 1864 declared a Free State

Maryland, my Maryland

My birthplace.

12-19-2020

Whiteford's Desire

I did not know this man, Hugh, my grandfather
six generations ago.

A lawyer, a farmer

Who enslaved, not hired.

Jane, Dina, Jess, Jean, and Jack.

Perspired.

Tired.

I do not know what transpired

Over the land called Whiteford's Desire.

12-19-2020

What do you like about being white?

What do you like about being white, she
asked?

Never until I embarked on a journey to
learn about whiteness and systemic racism,
did I ever consider this task.

Taking inventory of my ignorant white past.

Seeking knowledge on the impact of my
whiteness in contrast.

What I like about being white is so very
hard to define given the gained awareness
of the meaning of this color of mine.

What I like about being white is being on
the modern end on a line of a man who
fought for liberty during the Revolutionary
War, Private John Osborn.

What I like about being white I humbly say

Is that I am not necessitated to consider
my whiteness on any given day.

Now compelled by my raising awareness

I can't help but notice the unfairness.

What I like about being white is being a
part of the majority who together with
others can be an agent for social change
and more.

Combahee

Spending time at a modern-day pier.

The Combahee River Raid occurred here.

This gives me a shiver.

Where Harriet Tubman led a detachment of the Union
Army on steamships with her group of scouts.

The mission: carry troops to destroy plantations and
enslaved people to freedom deliver.

To freedom the people did shout.

The river and marsh are quiet today.

The sun reflects my shadow as the river reeds sway.

Cool air chills my face.

Vehicles traverse the Combahee on the Harriet Tubman
Memorial Bridge at a steady pace.

Do the travelers even realize the importance as they
pass through this historical place?

12-25-27-2020

ABOUT THE AUTHOR

Melissa Whiteford St. Clair hails from picturesque Harford County, Maryland. She married her high school sweetheart and for the next 30 years, home was where the U.S. Marine Corps sent them. Reflecting on the history of her home state and the history of her time spent in the lowcountry set the framework for this groundwork.

SPECIAL THANKS

To Joan H. Hodous, Artist, Author, Activist, Businesswoman, and Painter, for her appraisal of this little book of heartfelt poetry.

CONNECT ON SOCIAL

www.paperchaserbiz.com

www.linkedin.con/in/melissastclair

www.facebook.com/paperchaserbiz

www.pinterest.com/paperchaserbiz

www.youtube.com/c/PaperchaserbizVA
Biz/videos

IMAGE ACKNOWLEDGEMENTS

Trey Nelson, SoutherNothings-Unity photos

Learn more about the Unity Mural at https://www.centerforcreativepartnerships.org/projects

Author's photos

Harriet Tubman, Library of Congress 2018645050

Unity Mural, Beaufort, SC

www.ingramcontent.com/pod-product-compliance
Lightning Source LLC
Chambersburg PA
CBHW061146160726
48006CB00038B/2294